Ebenezer P Dorr

A Brief Sketch of the First Monitor and Its Inventor

A Paper Read Before the Buffalo Historical Society, January 5, 1874

Ebenezer P Dorr

A Brief Sketch of the First Monitor and Its Inventor
A Paper Read Before the Buffalo Historical Society, January 5, 1874

ISBN/EAN: 9783337010973

Printed in Europe, USA, Canada, Australia, Japan

Cover: Foto ©ninafisch / pixelio.de

A BRIEF SKETCH

OF

THE FIRST MONITOR

AND ITS INVENTOR:

A PAPER READ BEFORE THE

BUFFALO HISTORICAL SOCIETY,

JANUARY 5, 1874.

By EBEN. P. DORR.

PUBLISHED BY REQUEST.– SECOND EDITION.

BUFFALO, N. Y.

PRINTING HOUSE OF MATTHEWS & WARREN,

Office of the "Buffalo Commercial Advertiser."

1874.

THE FIRST MONITOR.

Mr. President and Gentlemen of the Buffalo Historical Society:

For the paper I am to read to-night I do not claim any literary merit. It is simply a mass of facts, connected with my subject, never presented by any other person, so far as I know. I have gathered the information principally from persons connected with and participating in the acts and scenes described; and shall endeavour to give them to you to-night, in my simple way, in connection with the illustrations here for that purpose, to show you the origin of the first "Monitor" and her subsequent career, down to the time of her being lost by foundering off Cape Hatteras.

In the progressive world at the present era, with the improvements that have been made in almost everything, and the great events that have crowded so thick and fast upon us for the past few years, there has been but little time to consider one idea, before another, often more startling than the other, has taken its place and the first is almost forgotten. This is especially true of this country. The Americans are in many respects a peculiar people; earnest, active, versatile; a moving, changing race; one sensation succeeding another in rapid succession. In no way has this been better illustrated than in the events that transpired during the late civil war. Coming upon us unexpectedly, and without preparation on the part of the North, the emergency had to be met, with an almost daily renewal of tact and invention on our part.

Among the great and stirring events of the war, none perhaps created more interest for the time being than the advent of the

"Monitor." Certainly nothing occurred during the war that exercised such a vast influence upon its ultimate results. What the battle of Gettysburg was to the Army at a later day, the fight between the "Monitor" and the "Merrimac" was to the Navy; both were turning points in the Rebellion. Under the gallant WORDEN the "Monitor" in 1862 fixed the boundaries of Rebellion by water at Hampton Roads; sixteen months later, the brave but now lamented MEADE, on the well-fought and bloody field of Gettysburg, with the chivalrous, often-whipped but never-daunted Army of the Potomac, fixed its boundaries by land beyond Pennsylvania. Both battles said to Rebellion, "Thus far shalt thou go, but no further;" removing the theatre of its action back upon the territory that originated it, and in the end crushing it forever.

In my opinion the people of this country have never attached sufficient importance to the advent and services of the first "Monitor," and the grand part she performed in the war, at an important crisis, when our very existence hung as it were upon a thread.

This much, Mr. President, by way of preface to my subject, "The First Monitor."

"MONITOR: One who warns of faults, or informs of duty. One who gives advice and instruction by way of reproof or caution."

After I had thus transcribed Webster's definition of the word "Monitor," I wrote to Mr. Ericsson, the inventor, asking him why his vessel was named "Monitor." He sent me in reply a copy of a letter he had written in answer to a request from the Navy Department to provide a name for his new invention, which I will give you in due order. First, however, I will read a copy of the contract to build the "Monitor," taken from a photographic copy, now in my possession, of the original contract, as executed by Messrs. Ericsson, Griswold and Winslow on one part, and Mr. Thos. F. Rowland on the other. Mr. C. S. Bushnell, of New Haven, was an associate contractor with Messrs. Ericsson, Griswold and Winslow, although his name does not appear on the original contract.

COPY OF CONTRACT.

This Agreement, made and entered into this twenty-fifth day of October, A. D. 1861, by and between Thomas F. Rowland, agent in behalf of the "Continental Iron Works," Green Point, Brooklyn, of the first part, and Capt. J. Ericsson of New York, Messrs. John F. Winslow and John A. Griswold of Troy, N. Y., and C. S. Bushnell of New Haven, Conn., parties of the second part.

Witnesseth: That the party of the first part for and in consideration of a certain sum hereinafter mentioned to be paid to him, by the parties of the second part, hereby covenants and agrees to furnish all the tools and facilities, and do all the labor necessary to execute the iron work of an Iron Battery Hull (it being understood that the new ship house now being erected is at the expense of the parties of the second part), said battery to be constructed from the plans and directions which have been or may be furnished the said party of the first part, by Captain Ericsson.

The party of the first part hereby further agrees to do the said work in a thorough and workmanlike manner, and to the entire satisfaction of Captain Ericsson, in the shortest possible space of time. And the party of the first part agrees to launch said battery safely and at his own risk and cost on the East River, then and there delivering her to the parties of the second part.

It is also understood that in consideration of the liberal price hereinafter stipulated to be paid by the party of the second part, that in case the work is not prosecuted with all the vigor and energy practicable, then and in that case Captain Ericsson is hereby empowered to instruct the party of the first part to employ a greater number of men or to work a greater number of hours, and which instruction the party of the first part hereby agrees to comply with in order that the work may be completed in the shortest possible space of time, as contemplated by his agreement.

The party of the second part hereby agrees to furnish all the material for the construction of said battery, delivering the same at the "Continental Iron Works" as soon as practicable, after receiving a specification of the materials required for the construction of said battery.

In consideration of the full and faithful performance of these presents by the party of the first part, the parties of the second part hereby covenant and agree to pay the party of the first part the sum of seven and one-half cents per pound (net weight) of iron used in the construction of said hull by the party of the first part.

Payments to be made weekly in proportion to the progress of the work; the balance remaining to be paid when the hull is launched.

The parties to this instrument hereby mutually agree, that should any alterations in the plan furnished by Captain Ericsson be desired after, the same have been executed, the party of the first part shall make any alterations that may be deemed desirable by Captain Ericsson at the expense of the parties of the second part.

Witness, the hands and seals of the said parties the day and year before written.

Witness to the signature of J. Ericsson, C. W. MacCord.	J. ERICSSON. [L. S.]
Witness to the signatures of J. F. Winslow and J. A. Griswold, F. Eus.	J. F. WINSLOW. [L. S.] JNO. A. GRISWOLD. [L. S.]
Witness to the signature of T. F. Rowland, Warren E. Hill.	T. F. ROWLAND. [L. S.]

The above contract with Mr. Rowland was based on one previously made by Messrs. Ericsson, Griswold, Winslow and Bushnell with the United States Government.

The hull of the "Monitor" was built by Mr. Rowland, from Capt. Ericsson's drawings and under his personal supervision, the materials (plates, bars, rivets, etc.) being furnished by his associates, Messrs. Griswold, Winslow and Bushnell. The turret was built at the Novelty Iron Works, according to his plans and under his supervision, with plates, rivets, etc., furnished by his associates. Being too heavy for transportation, it was taken down and placed in sections on the deck of a vessel, Mr. Rowland's men being employed to rivet the plates. The "port-stoppers" of the "Monitor" were made at the Steam Forge of Mr. Charles D. DeLancey, here, in Buffalo. They were made of heavy hammered wrought iron. After the guns were discharged and ran back into the turret, the "stoppers" swung over the port-holes of the turret, so as to prevent any shot from an enemy's ship from entering the port. The closing, regulated by machinery, was instantaneous, and that side of the turret swung away from the enemy; guns loaded, and again swung, and guns discharged, so that the ports were constantly protected, either by the guns obtruding or by the ports closed by the "stoppers."

Mr. DeLaney did a good deal of forging work for the Monitors subsequently built, obtained through Mr. Allan C. Stimers, Chief Engineer U. S. N., who had supervision of many of them.

The entire internal mechanism of the turret was built to Captain Ericsson's working plans, at the Delamater Iron Works, and put in place by Delamater's machinists. The steam machinery, boilers, propellers, etc., also designed by him, were likewise built at the Delamater Iron Works and put on board the vessel by Delamater's machinists. The wooden deck beams, side armor, timbers and decks were put up by Mr. Rowland, and the entire deck plating and side armor (furnished by Ericsson's associates) were attached by Rowland's men.

The mode of launching was planned by Mr. Rowland, evincing his great skill and experience. To prevent the vessel, when fully equipped with machinery, turret and armor, from plunging under water, Mr. Rowland constructed large wooden tanks, securing them under the stern. The launch, effected under his supervision, proved very successful.

Extraordinary diligence was displayed alike by Mr. Rowland, Mr. Delamater and the Novelty Iron Works. They all received payments in cash as the work progressed. The result of their joint efforts was that, within one hundred days from laying the keel plates of the hull, the whole work was completed and the engines of the vessel put in motion under steam ; probably the most expeditious work recorded in the annals of mechanical engineering.

The "Monitor" was launched on the 30th day of January, 1862, and her first trial trip and delivery to the Navy Yard was on February 19th, 1862. She had two trial trips afterwards, but was not in commission on her first trial trip, nor for some time—perhaps a week—afterwards. Captain Ericsson attended that trip. The vessel did not then attain the speed she did afterwards, because the cut-off valves had been set for running the engines backward, and would not admit the steam properly to the cylinders when going ahead. On the second trial trip, she was in commission under command of Lieut. Worden; but she could not be steered, and went no farther than the foot of Wall Street, New York. On the third trial trip, which occurred about March 4th, she went down to Sandy Hook and tried her guns, having a board of officers, consisting of Commodore Gregory, Chief Engineer Garvin and Constructor Hart, who reported favorably of her performance.

It should be stated here that when Captain Ericsson signed the contract with the Secretary of the Navy to furnish the turreted vessel (scarcely a week before laying the keel plates) he had completed only a small portion of the working drawings. Accordingly he had to make these during the stipulated one hundred days, preparing his plans and giving daily supervision to the work. His contract with the Government contained a distinct proviso that the entire structure should prove successful in practical operation, before the final payment; and in case of failure, himself and associates were liable to the Government for the entire amount advanced to them.

At this point it may be proper to state the origin of my interest in, and acquaintance with, "The First Monitor." A sailor in my early boyhood, and having been subsequently, in one way or another, always connected with ships and vessels, it has ever been my pleasure to examine, when in seaport towns, everything relating to ships and ship building. It has been my custom for many years, on my visits to New York City, to walk along the docks and to go into the ship-yards of that great commercial city. Walking down Twenty-third street one morning in the Winter of 1861–2, striking the East River and crossing over on the ferry-boat, a few minutes brought me to the Continental Iron Works, and without any knowledge of what was to be seen in the yard, I came upon what was afterwards known as the "Monitor," a name that was destined to electrify not only the American people but the whole civilized world. Before me were the first forgings of the iron foundation of this wonderful ship. That examination only stimulated me with a desire to know more of her, as the work progressed. My visits were so frequent, and my attention so close, that it excited the curiosity of one person, who was always there when I was. We were strangers, but one day he asked me my name, and my business there so often. In turn, Yankee like, I asked him the same question, and thus became acquainted with Thomas F. Rowland, proprietor of the Continental Iron Works, and builder of the first "Monitor."

And this was the way that he became the builder: The Continental Iron Works had been leased to two young men who had not made a success of the business, and one of whom was young Tom Rowland. The firm had been dissolved, and Rowland was asked by the kind-hearted owner, who wished to aid and encourage him, to take the Works and run them a year and see what he could make out of them. There he was, young Master Rowland, ready for work, and waiting like Micawber for something to turn up, when, one day, some gentlemen came into his Works looking around "to see what they could see," and, meeting Rowland, asked him what he would charge them a pound to build an iron ship, describing what they wanted as best they could. Rowland, who had never thought of the subject before, asked them what they expected to get it done for. His idea was to draw them out, to learn something of what was wanted and the price to be paid. After an interchange of views in this way, the strangers gave "four or four-and-a-half cents per pound" as the utmost price; they separated, neither party much the wiser for the interview. Those gentlemen were Messrs. Winslow and Griswold of Troy, and Mr. Bushnell of New Haven (whose names appear in the contract), self-made men, by honest, persistent, well-directed effort. Rich in this world's goods, but richer still in their great and noble natures, they wished to aid the great Ericsson with his invention, and were filled with patriotic anxiety for their country in her darkest hour, when she needed all possible aid to avert the impending downfall and ruin threatened by fratricidal strife. These were the men who furnished the means to build "the first Monitor."

Now let us look at another scene: In a room in New York City, with head and body bent over a drawing-table, surrounded by his papers and professional implements, was another person, the great Swede, Ericsson, plodding over his day and night dream, this iron-turreted Monitor; the man who first conceived the idea of building an iron-clad armored fighting ship of war that would be *invulnerable.* That Ericsson alone did this, long before it entered the head of any other person, is a fact well known to the civilized world.

The day following the visit of Messrs. Griswold, Winslow and Bushnell to Green Point, a message from the great naval architect, to whom the talent and ability of Tom Rowland was not unknown, brought him into Ericsson's presence at the latter's office. Just raising his head from the table, and casting his eye towards the door to know his visitor, and resuming his labor on the instant, not losing a moment from his great task, Ericsson said: "Tom, my boy, what are you going to charge me to build my iron ship?" Thinking of his interview of yesterday with the other parties, Tom answers at a venture, "Nine cents a pound." "Tut, tut, Tom!" cried Ericsson, his brain and hands still working on the problem before him, "it must be done for seven-and-a-half cents." And the trade was closed at that figure.

Now, gentlemen, here they are before you, the men who created this iron ship of war: Ericsson the inventor; Griswold, Winslow and Bushnell who furnished the means; with Rowland the builder: a ship of iron impregnability, that was to change the system of the naval warfare of the world. Let us here pause a moment to dwell on the foremost character.

John Ericsson was born in the Province of Vermland, in Sweden, on July 31st, 1803. Entered the Corps of Engineers of the

Royal Swedish Navy in 1815, as cadet. In 1819 he entered the Swedish Army and served under Bernadotte (Charles XIV.) during eight years, resigning his commission with the rank of Captain in 1827. Captain Ericsson is Chevalier of the Swedish Order of Vasa, and Knight Commander with the Grand Cross. He is Knight Commander of the Norwegian Order of Sanet Olaf, Knight Commander of the Danish Order of Dannebrog, first class, and Knight Commander of the Spanish Order of Isabella Catolica. He has also received the Rumford Medal, the great Gold Medal of the Mechanics' Institute of New York, the Medal of the Society of Arts in London, and several prize medals on both sides of the Atlantic. He is Doctor of Philosophy of the Royal University of Lund, in Sweden, Member of the Royal Academy of Sciences at Stockholm, Honorary Member of the Royal Academy of Military Sciences of Sweden, and member of many other scientific bodies in this country and in Europe, having likewise received the distinction of LL.D. from an American University.

For a while previous to 1839, Captain Ericsson was superintending Engineer in London of the Eastern Counties Railway, one of the principal lines centering in the British metropolis. He resigned that position and came to America under an arrangement with certain parties in this country to plan and superintend the construction of the machinery and armament of the U. S. steamship "Princeton." He landed at New York November 23d, 1839. His history for many years past is so well known, that it is needless here to recapitulate the details. For some time previous to 1854 his mind had dwelt upon the idea of planning and constructing an iron-plated shot-proof ship of war, and on the 26th of September, 1854, Captain Ericsson forwarded from New York to the Emperor Napoleon III. a plan of such a ship, with the following synopsis of his plans, showing conclusively, beyond all cavil, that America was the birth-place of the Monitor, and that John Ericsson was its sole inventor:

EXTRACT.

New System of Naval Attack.—The vessel to be composed entirely of iron. The midship section is triangular, with a broad, hollow keel, loaded to balance the heavy upper works. The ends of the vessel are moderately sharp. The deck, made of plate iron, is curved both longitudinally and transversely with a spring of five feet; it is made to project eight feet over the rudder and propeller. The entire deck is covered with a lining of sheet iron, three inches thick, with an opening in the center sixteen feet diameter. This opening is covered by a semi-globular turret of plate iron, six inches thick, revolving on a column and pivot by means of steam power and appropriate gear work. The vessel is propelled by a powerful steam engine, and *screw propeller.* Air for the combustion in the boilers, and for ventilation within the vessel, is supplied by a large self-acting centrifugal blower, the fresh air being drawn in through numerous small holes in the turret. The products of the combustion and impure air from the vessel is forced out through conductors leading to a cluster of small holes in the deck and turret. Surrounding objects are viewed through small holes at appropriate places. Reflecting telescopes, capable of being protruded or withdrawn at pleasure, also afford a distinct view of surrounding objects. The rudder stock passes through a water-tight stuffing box, so as to admit of the helm being worked within the vessel. Shot striking the deck are deflected, whilst shell exploding on it will prove harmless. Shot (of cast iron) striking the globular turret will crumble to pieces or are deflected. *This new system of naval attack will place an entire fleet of sailing ships, during calms and light winds, at the mercy of a single craft.** Boarding as a means of defence, will be impracticable, since the turret guns, which turn like the spokes in a wheel, commanding every point of the compass at once, may keep off and destroy any number of boats by firing slugs and combustibles.

A fleet at anchor might be fired and put in a sinking condition before enabled to get under way. Of what avail would be the "Steam Guard Ships" if attacked on the new system? Alas, for the "wooden walls" that formerly ruled the waves!

The long range Lancaster gun would scarcely hit the revolving iron turret once in six hours, and then, six chances to one, its shot or shell would be deflected by the varying angles of the face of the impregnable globe. When ultimately struck at right angles, the globe, which weighs upwards of forty tons, will be less affected by the shock than a heavy anvil by the blow of a light hammer; consequently, the shot would

*How prophetic!—E. P. D.

crumble to pieces, whilst the shell would strew the arched deck with harmless fragments.

During contest the revolving turret should be kept in motion, the port-holes being turned away from the opponent, except at the moment of discharge, which, however, should be made during full rotation, as the lateral aim in close quarters requires but little precision.

I would call your attention to the framed copy of the above described Ericsson's model of 1854. And please note how well the "Monitor" at Hampton Roads filled the predictions put forth at this time by Captain Ericsson!

Ericsson's letter was at once acknowledged by the Emperor, but, luckily for America, Napoleon did not embrace the opportunity of adopting for France, what, at a later day, at a most opportune moment, the great naval architect had the pleasure to first construct and put in use for the protection of his adopted country. All honor to the name of Ericsson! He will be remembered with gratitude in all coming time. In all naval history his name will be known as that of the greatest inventor and reformer in naval warfare that ever lived.

The trials and troubles Mr. Ericsson experienced, even with the aid of Bushnell, Winslow and Griswold, to get his "Monitor" adopted by the Government, no one but himself and associates can ever know. But by the individual, persevering efforts of the great inventor, with the assistance of these good friends, and guided by the great Director of all things, it was finally accomplished, just in time to save this nation.

Now I will give you the promised letter, explaining why Ericsson gave his ship the name "Monitor."

(COPY.)

NEW YORK, Jan. 20th, 1862.

SIR,—In accordance with your request, I now submit for your approbation a name for the floating battery at Green Point.

The impregnable and aggressive character of this structure will admonish the leaders of the Southern Rebellion that the batteries on the banks of their rivers will no longer present barriers to the entrance of the Union forces.

The iron-clad intruder will thus prove a severe monitor to those leaders. But there are other leaders who will also be startled and admonished by the booming of the guns from the impregnable iron turret. "Downing Street" will hardly view with indifference this last "Yankee notion," this monitor. To the Lords of the Admiralty the new craft will be a monitor, suggesting doubts as to the propriety of completing those four steel-clad ships at three-and-a-half millions a piece.

On these and many similar grounds I propose to name the new battery "Monitor."

Your obedient servant, J. ERICSSON.

To GUSTAVUS V. FOX, Ass't Sec'y of the Navy.

The "Monitor" was wanted quickly; there was not a minute to lose. All the force that could work on her was employed; night and day the work was driven. The plans and designs were worked up and applied as fast as the material could be procured and formed. Not a moment too soon was she completed and hurried off. After two very slight trial trips to sea, she was on her great mission to Fortress Monroe, in which vicinity she was so much needed.

The manning of the "Monitor" with her crew was, to me, one of the most interesting events connected with this wonderful craft. Here was a hitherto unknown and untried vessel, with all but a small portion of her below the water,—not floating upon the water as other vessels were supposed to do, but nearly submerged,—her crew to live, if live they could, below the surface; the ocean beating with its wild and restless waves right over their heads. There was something calmly and terribly heroic in the act of manning this iron coffin-like ship. Let me give you the history of furnishing her with a crew.

Lieutenant Worden, U. S. N., was ordered to command her. When she was nearly ready for commission, he was authorized by the Navy Department to select a crew from the receiving ship "North Carolina," or any other vessel of war in the harbor of New York. Under that authority he asked for volunteers from the "North Carolina" and frigate "Sabine." After stating fully to the crews of these vessels the probable dangers of the passage to Hampton Roads, and the certainty of having important

services to perform there, he had many more volunteers than was required. From them he selected a crew, and a better one, he said, no naval commander ever had the honor to command.

History ought to preserve the names of the gallant men who voluntarily stepped out, and asked to be permitted to serve their country in her hour of greatest need, by going on board —no! not "on board" ship, as it is usually termed, but into this almost hermetically-sealed unknown ship, shut out from the light of God's sun and from the air above the sea, depending entirely upon artificial means to supply the air to breathe, to sustain life. A failure of the machinery to do this when in rough water was almost certain and speedy death. You will see how near it came to that, on her first passage from New York.

In the sinking of the English troop ship off the Cape of Good Hope, we read what discipline and training will do with brave men in imminent peril, when facing apparent instant death. The men were ordered to "fall in," stepping out in full dress, arms in hand, forming in line as though at dress parade upon the deck of the sinking ship, going down at their posts without breaking ranks. And we read of the gallant sentry on the sinking "Oneida," who would not leave his post until the order came from the corporal relieving him. No order came, and he went down with the ship, sacrificing his life to discipline and duty.

History furnishes many similar cases of heroic men, who have deemed the higher order of duty and self-sacrificing principle superior to their love of life. But to me, these men, comfortably housed on the receiving ship, volunteering for this special dangerous and unknown service, afford an example of patriotic devotion far superior to the above cases.

For the officers that manned the "Monitor" let me say: they showed what routine discipline, as taught in our National Naval School, will do for the Navy; just as West Point has done for the Army. (I say this without a word of disparagement or detraction of services of our gallant volunteers of the Navy or Army.) Their action teaches us that knowledge is power. They go where duty calls them, quietly, without a murmur.

The whole record of the Rebellion, on both sides, is full of a perfect vindication of the great value of both of these cherished institutions.

Lieutenant Worden was ordered to command the "Monitor" on January 13th, 1862, when she was still on the stocks. Prior to that date, Lieutenant S. D. Greene had interested himself in her, and thoroughly examined her construction, design, and qualities. Notwithstanding the many gloomy predictions of naval officers, and officers of the mercantile marine, as to the great probability of her sinking at sea, Greene volunteered to go in her, and, at Worden's request, he was directed to do so. From the date of his orders he applied himself unremittingly and intelligently to the study of the "Monitor's" peculiar requirements, and to her fitting and equipment. She was put in commission early in February, 1862, and from that time until her day of sailing, Commander Worden, Lieutenant Greene and all the officers and crew displayed untiring energy and zeal in getting her ready, and in the conduct of the several trials of her engines, turret machinery, etc. The "Monitor" was finished on February 20th, 1862, and Commander Worden received his sailing orders as follows:

ORDERS FOR THE "MONITOR" TO PROCEED TO HAMPTON ROADS, VA.

NAVY DEPARTMENT, February 20th, 1862.

SIR,—Proceed with the U. S. steamer "Monitor" under your command to Hampton Roads, Va., and on your arrival there, report by letter to the Department.

Commodore Paulding has been instructed to charter a vessel to accompany the "Monitor," provided none of our vessels are going South about the time she sails.

Transmit to the Department a muster roll of the crew and a separate list of the officers of the "Monitor," before sailing from New York.

I am respectfully, your obedient servant,

(Signed) GIDEON WELLES.

To Lieut. JOHN L. WORDEN, U. S. N.,
Commanding U. S. Iron Clad Steamer "Monitor," New York.

He hastened with all due diligence to get ready, but something about the steering apparatus, and other matters, detained him from going to sea for some days. On the 4th of March, he received orders from the officer commanding the Navy Yard at New York, which read as follows:

NAVY YARD, NEW YORK, March 4th, 1862.

Lieut. Commanding JOHN L. WORDEN, *U. S. Str. "Monitor:"*

SIR,—When the weather permits, you will proceed with the "Monitor" under your command to Hampton Roads, and on your arrival report to the Senior Naval Officer there.

I have hired the steamer "James Freeborn" to tow the "Monitor," and have also directed the propellers "Sachem" and "Currituck" to attend on you to the mouth of the Chesapeake. If it should be necessary to retain them longer, you are authorized to do so.

When you shall have no further use or occasion for the "Freeborn," be pleased to give the Captain a certificate, with directions to return to New York, and immediately on his arrival report to me.

Wishing you a safe and successful passage,

I am, respectfully, your ob'd't servant,

H. PAULDING,

Commander.

The "Monitor" left the Lower Bay of New York on the afternoon of the 6th day of March, 1862, with a moderate wind from the westward and smooth sea, in tow of a small tug, the "Seth Low," and accompanied by the U. S. steamers "Currituck" and "Sachem." About mid-day of the 7th, the wind had freshened to a strong breeze, causing, in their then position off the Capes of the Delaware, a rough sea, which broke constantly and violently over her decks, and forcing the water in considerable quantities into the vessel, through the hawse-pipes, under the turret, and in various other places. About four o'clock P. M., the wind and sea still increasing, the water broke over the smoke and blower pipes (the former six feet and the latter four feet high), which, wetting the blower bands, caused them to slip and finally to break. The blowers being thus stopped, there was no draft for the furnaces, and the engine and fire rooms became immediately filled with gas. The senior engineer, Mr. Isaac Newton, and his assistants, met the emergency with great determination, but were unable to stand the gas, which in a very short time prostrated them, apparently lifeless, upon the floor of the engine-room, from which they were rescued and carried to the top of the turret, where they finally revived.

With the motive power thus useless for propulsion or for pumping, the water, which was entering the vessel in many places, was increasing rapidly. The hand pumps were used, and men set to work bailing, but with little effect. The tug-boat having the "Monitor" in tow was ordered to head directly in shore; but being light and of moderate power, she could move the "Monitor" but slowly against wind and sea. Between seven and eight o'clock, however, they got into smoother water, and were enabled to so far clear the engine-room of gas as to permit the blower bands to be repaired and the blower to be set in motion. By eight o'clock they were on their course again, with the engines going slowly, in a comparatively smooth sea. This lasted until shortly after midnight, when, in crossing a shoal, the sea suddenly became rough again, broke violently over the deck, causing fears of another disaster to the blowers. The wheel ropes too became jammed, and for half an hour, until, it was cleared, the vessel yawed unmanageably, seriously endangering the towing-hawser, which fortunately held, and in a short time they were clear of the shoal and in smooth water again.

From this time no further serious mishap occurred. About four o'clock P. M. of Saturday, March 8th, they passed Cape Henry light, and soon after heard heavy firing in the direction of Fortress Monroe, indicating an engagement, which they rightly concluded to be with the "Merrimac," as they had been informed of her preparation to get to sea.

Lieutenant Worden immediately ordered the vessel to be stripped of her sea rig, the turret to be keyed up, and in every way to be prepared for action. About midway between Cape Henry and Fortress Monroe, a pilot boat came along and gave them a pilot, from whom they learned of the advent of the "Merrimac," the disaster to the ships "Cumberland" and "Congress," and the generally gloomy condition of affairs in Hampton Roads.

At this point let me give you a history of the destruction of the U. S. ships "Cumberland" and "Congress" by the rebel ram "Merrimac," on the 8th day of March, 1862. The ships lay about one-quarter of a mile apart, and as far from the shore off Newport News, at anchor. On the Monday previous, Captain Radford (now Admiral), commanding the "Cumberland," left for Old Point, where he was ordered, as president of a court-martial, on board the "Roanoke." Lieut. Geo. Morris, the Executive Officer, was left in command. Imagine the description as made from the decks of the "Cumberland."

On Saturday, at eleven o'clock A. M., March 8th, 1862, the "Merrimac" was reported coming around the Point from Norfolk. She was accompanied by the "Frazer" and "Yorktown," two small steamers armed with rifled guns. On the "Cumberland" and "Congress" they beat to quarters. Their pilot seeing the "Merrimac" keep in close to the opposite shore, thought she had missed the channel. It has since been ascertained that she found a new channel. At first all officers were allowed on the spar deck; but as she neared them, all went to their stations. I cannot state the exact hour at which the "Merrimac" opened fire on the "Cumberland," but it was at dead slack water, Commander Buchanan of the "Merrimac" having chosen that time to attack, as the "Cumberland" and "Congress," being sailing ships, could not at slack water use springs on their cables to present their broadsides to the approaching enemy. The crafty Buchanan well knew this (his own brother was an officer on one of the Union ships), and he selected this opportune hour to attack, bow on, taking the "Cumberland" at the greatest possible disadvantage, when she could hardly train a gun to bear upon her formidable antagonist.

A small tug, the "Zouave," built and previously used to tow boats under the grain elevator in the basin at Albany, N. Y., had been detailed to assist in case of an attack. The "Congress," the senior ship, commanded by Lieut. Joseph Smith temporarily (her Captain—also a Smith—had been detached the day before, but was on board at the time and acted as a volunteer in the fight), slipped her chains. It was a dead calm. She made fast to the "Zouave" and attempted to meet the "Merrimac." The "Zouave" broke down, was cast adrift and floated away, firing her small pop-gun at the "Merrimac." The "Congress" grounded. The "Merrimac" stood for the "Cumberland," and opened fire upon her. The first shot killed and wounded ten men of the after pivot gun. Her second shot killed and wounded twelve men at the forward pivot gun. Her two tenders at the same time fired percussion shells into the "Cumberland." The "Merrimac" then rammed her, striking her on the starboard bow.

I now quote in substance from an officer on board the "Cumberland":

"I was looking through the air port of the sick bay, at the time, and had a full view of the "Merrimac." She was like a long iron shed sunk down to the roof, with a gun put in the gable. The shock was not great. I heard the stones rattling in the gunners' room underneath, and some of the bolts in the hanging knees were driven in, and the water spouted in, in a full stream. Part of the wounded had been brought down and were partially dressed, when a percussion shell came through the spar deck hatch, bursting in the sick bay immediately under the spar deck, killing four of the wounded men. By this time the ship was settling by the head, and we moved to the steerage. It was necessary to lift the wounded, brought down to the berth deck, on to the big racks and mess-chests, to save them from drowning in the water, which was making very fast.

"All this time the three rebel ships continued to fire on us, and it was as warmly returned. Trunks of cartridges were hoisted on the gun deck and opened, the guns crews kicked off their shoes, stripped to their pants, their heads tied up with their black neck handkerchiefs, loaded, fired, yelled, and dragged the killed and wounded amidships. There was no time for form, or to send them below.

"In forty-five minutes from the time she was struck, the order was given to leave quarters and save themselves as best they could. The ship, in sinking, heeled over. The ladders were almost perpendicular. The crash was fearful. As there is often in the gravest scenes a corner for the ludicrous, so there was in this. The marine drummer holding on to his drum, the men pushing him up behind from below, landing him on deck with it, caused a laugh at his expense, desperately as we were situated.

"When the spar deck was reached, it inclined like the roof of a house. The boats, previous to the action, had all been lowered and made fast in a line on the shore side. Every one took to the water and swam for the boats. While hesitating at the after pivot port, a man next me said, 'Jump! here comes the pivot gun.' It had been pivoted on the upper side, and breaking away, rushed down in the water, catching, as it went, Quartermaster Murray, a young, active, unwounded man. He fell, and the gun bounded on his back, like some fierce animal, breaking his spine. His face rose with an unutterable look of agony, which once seen can never be forgotten.

"The ship sunk to her tops, in which many of the men took refuge. As the boats made for the shore, the enemy continued to shell us, but we were below in the water, so that the shell went over us. One of them knocked to pieces the end of the wharf we were making for. On landing, the soldiers met us in crowds; they hugged and embraced us, and whiskey flasks were held to our mouths, plugs of tobacco shoved into our pockets, and they cried and cheered and cursed; and we were clothed and comforted by them.

"The "Cumberland" lost one hundred and seventeen out of three hundred. Fourteen of the wounded were saved. When the order was given to leave the ship, the wounded men, most of them mangled by shell, begged to be killed rather than be left to drown, and the yell of agony as she sank was heard in the camp of the troops on shore. But *she sank with her colors flying!*

"The last gun was fired by a volunteer officer, Lieut. Randall, now in the naval service. Lieut. Morris was hailed by Captain Buchanan of the "Merrimac," 'Do you surrender?' He answered, 'No, sir!'

"The slaughter was terrible among the marines. They were commanded by Lieut. Charles Heywood, a gallant man. There were many interesting scenes on board. A man dreadfully, hopelessly wounded, had been carried down to the cock-pit.

While therein, his 'chummy,' or friend, with a wounded hand, came to have it dressed, intending to return. The wounded man said, 'Tom, are you going to leave me?' Tom said, 'No, I will not!' and sat down on deck, took his friend's head in his lap and went down with him. The cock-pit sentry also went down at his post.

"Leaving the "Cumberland," the ram went for the "Congress." She was aground and helpless. Hot shot were fired into her, and she was soon on fire. Full of wounded men, Lieut. Smith killed, the ship on fire, she surrendered. A small tender from the "Merrimac" went between her and the shore, but the Zouaves under Col. Lozier with their rifles picked off the men in the tug, and she left without making a prisoner or securing the *flag* of the "Congress;" and then, to the surprise of every one, the "Merrimac" steamed back for Norfolk. She had left the ram in the "Cumberland," and was leaking badly. All the wounded of the "Congress" were taken ashore, and at 12.30 she blew up, the fire having reached her magazines.

"An old man, Russell, aged sixty, stationed in the after magazine of the "Cumberland," went down with the ship, made his way up through the hatches to the surface and was hauled into the mizzen-top, the only one out of water. The weight rushing forward kept her head lower than the stern, entirely submerging the fore and main tops. As soon as Captain Radford heard the firing he attempted to reach us; but the "Roanoke" was repairing her machinery, the "Minnesota" aground, and, as we landed at Newport News, he rode down to the beach on a horse without saddle or bridle, merely a halter. He was ragged and muddy from falls, haggard with anxiety and regret; but brightened up when he was pointed to the flag still flying on his ship! He was noted for complete control of himself, but he cried like a child when contemplating the sad scene before him. A kinder and braver Captain never commanded a ship, and though he regretted his own absence, he approved the acts of the gallant Morris, his officers and crew, by saying: 'It could not have been done better.'"

Gentlemen, you have thus the simple touching story of the sinking and burning of the "Cumberland" and "Congress." History does not record a more glorious desperate fight, than was fought by their gallant crews on our side, or a meaner and more despicable one on the part of the enemy. It demonstrated also the destructive powers of the "Merrimac."

Sunday morning (the 9th of March) the return of the "Merrimac" was reported in camp at Newport News, and also a second message, to the effect that the strangest-looking craft was in sight. She had been hidden by the hull of the "Minnesota," which ship attempted on Saturday to assist us; but was run on a shoal and was left a fair target for the ram, and it was to destroy her they came out that Sunday. Then began the first iron-clad fight.

We will again resume the story of the "Monitor."

About nine P. M. of the 8th of March she anchored near the frigate "Roanoke," Captain Marston (the senior officer present), to whom Lieutenant Worden reported, and who suggested that he should go to the assistance of the frigate "Minnesota," then aground off Newport News. Finding difficulty in getting a pilot, Worden accepted the services of Acting-Master Samuel Howard, who earnestly volunteered for that service. Under his pilotage the "Monitor" reached the "Minnesota" about half-past eleven o'clock P. M., when Worden reported to Captain Van Brunt, her commanding officer, and anchored near the "Minnesota," at about one o'clock Sunday morning, March 9th.

They hoped to get the "Minnesota" afloat at high water, about two o'clock following, but failed to do so. At daylight the "Merrimac" was discovered, with several consorts, at anchor under Sewell's Point. Lieutenant Worden went at once to see Captain Van Brunt, whose vessel was still aground, greatly damaged from the attack of the day before, and in a helpless condition. After a few minutes conversation with him relative to the situation of affairs, Worden left, telling Captain Van Brunt he would develop all the qualities, offensive and defensive, possessed by the battery under his command, to protect his vessel (the "Minnesota") from the attack of the "Merrimac," should she come out again, and that he (Worden) had great faith in her capabilities. Shortly afterwards he returned to the "Monitor," and at about half-past seven o'clock A. M. the "Merrimac" was observed to be approaching, accompanied by her consorts, steaming slowly. The "Monitor" got under way as soon as possible, and stood directly for the "Merrimac," with crew at quarters, in order to meet or engage her as far away from the "Minnesota" as possible. As they approached the enemy, her wooden consorts turned and stood back in the direction from which they had come, and she turned her head up stream, against the tide, remaining nearly stationary, and commenced firing.

At this time, about eight o'clock A. M., the "Monitor" was approaching the "Merrimac" on her starboard bow, on a course nearly at right angles with her line of keel, the "Monitor" reserving fire, until near enough that every shot might take effect. She continued to so approach until within very short range, when she altered her course parallel with the "Merrimac," but with bows in opposite directions. Then the "Monitor" stopped her engine and commenced firing. In this way she passed slowly by the "Merrimac," within a few yards, delivering her fire as rapidly as possible, and receiving from the "Merrimac" a rapid fire in return, both from her great guns and musketry, the latter aimed at the pilot-house, hoping, undoubtedly, to penetrate it through the look-out holes and to disable the commanding officer, pilot and helmsman, the sole occupants. At this moment Worden felt some anxiety about the turret machinery, it having been predicted by many persons that a heavy shot striking the turret with great initial velocity would so derange it as to stop its working; but, finding that it had been twice struck and still revolved as freely as ever, he turned back with renewed confidence and hope, and continued the engagement at close quarters; every shot from the "Monitor's" guns taking effect upon the huge sides of her adversary, stripping off the iron plating freely.

During the engagement, the "Monitor" ran across and close to the stern of the "Merrimac," hoping to disable her screw, which she could not have missed by more than two feet.

After having passed up on her port side, in crossing her bow to get between her and the "Minnesota" again, the "Merrimac" steamed up quickly, and finding that she would strike the "Monitor" with her prow or ram, Worden put the "Monitor's" helm "hard a port," giving a broad sheer with her bow towards the enemy's stern, thus avoiding a direct blow and receiving it at a sharp angle on the starboard quarter, which caused it to glance off without inflicting any injury to the "Monitor."

The contest so continued, except for an interval of about fifteen minutes, when the "Monitor" hauled off to remedy some deficiency in the supply of shot in the turret, until near noon, when, being within ten yards of the enemy, a shell from the "Merrimac" struck her pilot-house near the look-out hole, through which Worden was looking. The shell exploded, fracturing one of the logs of iron of which it was composed, filling his face and eyes with powder, utterly blinding and partially stunning him. His escape from instant death was marvelous, as I heard from his own lips. He had just at that moment withdrawn his face from immediate contact with the look-out hole; if he had kept it there a moment longer, the shell that disabled would have killed him outright. (I would here state that Mr. Ericsson improved very much afterwards upon the pilot-houses; those of the present day are quite different affairs from that of the first "Monitor.")

The top of the pilot-house was partially lifted off by the force of the concussion, which let in a flood of light so strong as to be apparent to Worden, blind as he was, and caused him to believe that the pilot-house was seriously disabled. He therefore gave orders to put the helm to starboard and sheer off, and sent for Lieutenant Greene and directed him to take command. Worden was then taken to his quarters, and had been there but a short time when it was reported to him that the "Merrimac" was retiring in the direction of Norfolk.

In the meantime, Lieut. Greene, after taking his place in the pilot-house and finding the injuries there less serious than Worden supposed, had turned the vessel's head again in the direction of the enemy to continue the engagement; but before he could get at close quarters with her, the "Merrimac" retired.

He, therefore, very properly returned to the "Minnesota," and lay by her until she floated.

The "Merrimac" having been thus checked in her career of destruction and driven back crippled and discomfited, the question arises, Should she have been followed in her retreat to Norfolk? That such a course would commend itself very temptingly to the gallantry of an officer and be difficult to resist, is undeniable; yet I am convinced that, under the condition of affairs then existing at Hampton Roads, with the great interests at stake there, all of which were entirely dependent upon the "Monitor," good judgment forbade a pursuit of the enemy. It must be remembered that the pilot-house of the "Monitor" was situated well forward in her bows, and that it was considerably damaged. In following in the wake of the enemy, in order to fire clear of the pilot-house it would have been necessary to make broad "yaws" to starboard or port, involving, in the excitement of such a chase, the very serious danger of grounding the "Monitor" in the narrower portions of the channels, and near some of the enemy's batteries, whence it would have been very difficult to extricate her, and possibly involving her loss. Such a danger her commander would not, in my judgment, have been justified in encountering: for her loss would have left the vital interests in all the waters of the Chesapeake at the mercy of future attacks from the "Merrimac." Had there been another iron-clad in reserve at that point to guard those interests, the question would have presented a different aspect; one that would not only have justified him in following the retreating enemy, but perhaps made it his imperative duty to do so.

The fact that the battle with the "Merrimac" was not more decided was due to the want of knowledge of the endurance of the eleven-inch Dahlgren guns, with which the "Monitor" was armed, and which had not been fully tested. Just before leaving New York, Lieutenant Worden received a peremptory order from the Bureau of Ordnance, to use only the prescribed service charge, viz., fifteen pounds, and he did not feel justified in violating those instructions at the risk of bursting one of the guns, an accident which, placed as they were in the turret, would have almost entirely disabled the vessel. Had he been able to use the thirty-pound charges which experience has since shown the guns to be capable of enduring, there is little doubt in my mind that the contest would have been shorter and the result more decisive.

Further, the crew had been but a few days on board, the weather was bad, mechanics had been at work on her up to the moment of sailing, and sufficient opportunity had not been afforded to practice with the guns, the mode of manipulating which was entirely novel. A few days at Hampton Roads for drilling the men and getting the guns and turret-gear in smooth-working order (the latter, from having been constantly wet on the passage, was somewhat rusted), would have enabled the guns to have been handled more quickly and effectively, and with better results.

In his official report Lieutenant Worden said that he desired to express his high approbation of the zeal, energy and courage displayed by every officer and man under his command during this remarkable combat, as well as during the trying scenes of the passage from New York. He commended one and all most heartily to the favorable consideration of the Department and of the country. Lieutenant Greene, the executive officer, had charge of the turret, and handled the guns with great courage, coolness and skill. Throughout the engagement, as well as in the equipment of the vessel, and on her passage to Hampton Roads, he exhibited an earnest devotion to duty, unsurpassed in Lieutenant Worden's experience. For which good service Worden had the honor in person, about seven years ago, to recommend Greene to the Department and to the Board of Admirals for advancement, in accordance with the precedent established in the case of Lieutenant Commander Thornton, the executive officer of the "Kearsage," in her memorable fight with the "Alabama."

Acting-Master Samuel Howard, who volunteered as pilot, stood by Lieutenant Worden in the pilot-house, during the engagement, and behaved with courage and coolness. For his services on that occasion he has since been promoted to Acting Volunteer Lieutenant.

Chief Engineer A. C. Stimers, U. S. N., made the passage on the vessel, to report upon the performance of the machinery, and performed useful service during the engagement, in manipulating the turret. He was the only volunteer, outside of the crew, that left New York on the "Monitor." Mr. Ericsson speaks of him in such high terms in fitting out the "Monitor," and Admiral Worden commends him so much for his services during the fight, that I deem him worthy of more than a passing notice here. Mr. Stimers was born in the township of Smithfield, Madison County, N. Y., June 5th, 1827. He was educated in the common schools of the State, with six months in a select school in the village of Byron Centre, Genesee County, N. Y. He learned the machinist's trade, and entered the Navy as Third Assistant Engineer, June 11th, 1849, and became Chief Engineer in 1858. He was married in Buffalo, November 25, 1852, to the adopted daughter of the late Gilman Appleby, and was living here with his family when the war broke out in 1861, having just returned from the Pacific, where he had been cruising as Chief Engineer of the flag-ship "Merrimac." He served as Assistant Engineer of the "Michigan," on the Lakes during 1850, 1851 and 1852.

I append Mr. Stimer's account of the "Monitor's" first voyage to Hampton Roads, with report of the engagement, and her subsequent loss, and the cause of it, off Cape Hatteras.

First Assistant Engineer Isaac Newton, the Chief Engineer of the vessel, and his assistants, managed the machinery with careful skill, and gave prompt and correct attention to all the signals from the pilot-house. Acting Assistant Paymaster W. F. Keeler and Captain's Clerk Daniel Toffey made their services very useful in transmitting the orders of Lieutenant Worden to the turret. Peter Williams, Quarter-Master, was at the helm by the side of Worden, and won his admiration by his cool and steady handling of the wheel.

I will here give the crew list, which has never been made public before. Fifty-seven men of crew proper, and with Mr. Stimers (volunteer), fifty-eight manned the "Monitor."

LIST OF THE OFFICERS AND CREW OF THE U. S. S. "MONITOR."

Lieut. John L. Worden, U. S. N.,	Commanding.
Lieut. Samuel D. Greene, U. S. N.,	Executive Officer.
Louis N. Stodder,	Master.
John J. N. Webber,	Master.
Daniel C. Logne,	Assistant Surgeon.
W. F. Keeler,	Paymaster.
Isaac Newton,	First Assistant Engineer.
Albert B. Campbell,	Second Assistant Engineer.
R. W. Hands,	Third Assistant Engineer.
M. T. Sunstrum,	Third Assistant Engineer.
Daniel Toffey,	Captain's Clerk.
Geo. Frederickson,	Acting Master's Mate.
Jesse M. Jones,	Hospital Steward.
R. R. Hubbell,	Paymaster's Steward.
Richard Angier,	Quarter-Master.
Peter Williams,	Quarter-Master.
Moses M. Stearns,	Quarter-Master.
Derick Brinkman,	Carpenter's Mate.
Robert Williams,	First Class Fireman.
John Driscoll,	First Class Fireman.
Abram Fester,	First Class Fireman.
Wm. Richardson,	First Class Fireman.
George S. Geer,	First Class Fireman.
Patrick Hannan,	First Class Fireman.
Mathew Leonard,	First Class Fireman.
Thomas Joyce,	First Class Fireman.
John Garrety,	First Class Fireman.
Edmund Brown,	First Class Fireman.
Joseph Crown,	Gunner's Mate.
John Rooney,	Master at Arms.
Thomas Carroll, 1st,	Captain of Hold.
John P. Conklin,	Quarter Gunner.
John Stocking,	Boatswain's Mate.
Lawrence Murray,	Landsman.
Wm. H. Nichols,	Landsman.
William Byran,	Yeoman.
David Cuddebuck,	Officers' Steward.
Edward Moore,	Officers' Cook.
Thomas Longhran,	Ship's Cook.
Thomas Carroll, 2d,	First Class Boy.
Charles F. Sylvester,	Seaman.

Charles Peterson, ...	Seaman.
Anton Basting, ...	Seaman.
Hans Anderson, ...	Seaman.
Peter Truscott, ...	Seaman.
Thomas B. Vial, ...	Seaman.
William Marion, ...	Seaman.
Anthony Connoly, ...	Seaman.
James Fenwick, ...	Seaman.
Daniel Welch, ...	Seaman.
Michael Mooney, ...	Coal Heaver.
Ellis Roberts, ...	Coal Heaver.
William Durst, ...	Coal Heaver.
James Seery, ...	Coal Heaver.
Robert Quinn, ...	Coal Heaver.
John Mason, ...	Coal Heaver.
Christy Price, ...	Coal Heaver.

A. C. Stimers, Chief Engineer, passenger, and volunteer officer.

Mr. President and gentlemen, the battle of the "Monitor" and "Merrimac" is over. The once proud, and supposed invincible and invulnerable, ship has retired, battered and worthless, never again to fire a hostile gun aimed at the flag from which she rebelled and was stolen.

The prophecy of Ericsson as to what his "Monitor" could do has been fulfilled. She has been "heard from." In Downing Street by the Lords of Admiralty; by peasant and peer alike, all over the world, wherever language is printed or written, Ericsson and his "Monitor" have been heard of. Their triumph has been complete.

Captain Ericsson received a vote of thanks from Congress, couched in very flattering terms, as follows:

Resolved, by the Senate and House of Representatives of the United States of America, in Congress assembled: That it is fit and proper that a public acknowledgment be made to Captain John Ericsson for the enterprise, skill, energy and forecast displayed by him in the construction of his iron-clad boat, the "Monitor," which, under gallant and able management, came so opportunely to the rescue of our fleet in Hampton Roads, and perchance, of all our coast defences near, and arrested the work of destruction then being successfully prosecuted by the enemy, by their iron-clad steamer, seemingly irresistible by any other power at our command, and that the thanks of Congress are hereby presented to him for the great service he has thus rendered to the country.

The Legislature of this State also passed a vote of thanks which was inscribed on parchment, set in a fine gilt frame, the "Monitor" and its constructor being truthfully depicted. A committee of six members of the Legislature being appointed to present to him this valuable document, which read as follows:

State of New York, in Assembly, March 13th, 1862.

Whereas, The recent naval engagement in Hampton Roads, while establishing the utility and importance of iron-clad vessels of war, has equally confirmed the genius of our inventors, and the undaunted gallantry of our naval officers and sailors; therefore, be it

Resolved, That John Ericsson, in the conception and construction of the "Monitor," has materially contributed to the protection of our forces on sea and land, and the effective and speedy prosecution of the war; and is eminently entitled to the thanks of his countrymen.

Some leading engineering establishments and ship builders also presented him with a magnificent model of the "Monitor," made of pure gold, weighing upwards of fourteen pounds, the entire detail of the turret machinery, &c., being represented, and is said to have cost seven thousand dollars.

Here I will give you a list of the ships and guns that were afloat in Hampton Roads on that memorable Sunday morning, March 9th, 1862, and then sum up the result.

Twenty ships of war in all, mounting 298 guns, headed by the "Monitor," viz.:

"Monitor," . . .	mounting	2	guns.	
"Roanoke," . . .	"	40	"	
"Minnesota," . . .	"	48	"	
"Congress," . . .	"	50	"	
"Cumberland," . .	"	24	"	
"St. Lawrence," . .	"	50	"	
"Brandywine," . .	"	50	"	Store Ship.
"Ben Morgan," . .	"	no	"	Ordnance ship.
"Cambridge," . . .	"	5	"	
"Whitehall," . .	"	2	"	Tug.

"Mount Vernon," .	mounting	3 guns.	
"Mystic," . . .	"	4 "	
"Dragon," .	"	1 "	Tug.
"Zouave," . . .	"	1 "	Tug.
"Mount Washington," .	"	4 "	
"Braziliera," . . .	"	6 "	
"S. R. Spaulding," . .	"	3 "	
"Young America," . .	"	2 "	Tug.
"Charles Phelps," . .	"	1 "	
"Delaware," . . .	"	2 "	
		298 guns.	

There were also a number of transports, chartered vessels and private property, swelling to a large amount the values of life and property exposed to the "Merrimac." This all captured and destroyed, the Atlantic seaboard cities were at the mercy of the famous rebel ram, and no estimate could be made of her powers of destruction. The "Monitor" saved them all. If she had not won, European governments would have acknowleged the Confederacy at once.

In reference to the first mission of the "Monitor," there is a little bit of history that is worthy of special mention. I have already shown that Lieutenant Worden was directed to proceed to Hampton Roads for orders. Two hours after he had sailed from New York, orders came from Washington directing him to proceed to the Potomac, where it was thought the "Monitor" was more needed, leaving the large fleet of war vessels at Hampton Roads to protect that place. The authorities little dreamed then of the aggressive powers of the "Merrimac," and how poorly the whole fleet was prepared to cope with that powerful antagonist. Luckily, Worden and his "Monitor" were beyond its reach. But can we call it luck? Was it not rather the special interposition of Divine Providence to save the great cities of the Atlantic seaboard from certain destruction by the "Merrimac," after she had destroyed every vessel in Hampton Roads? Considering the timely appearance of our "Monitor," who can doubt that we were cared for by the great Director of all things.

The above fact came to my knowledge quite recently, since the greater portion of this paper was written, and it is added as another of the many wonderful incidents connected with the subject.

You can see here before you a perfect miniature scale-model of the "Monitor," made at Mr. Rowland's "Continental Iron Works" at Green Point. Her subsequent career was as follows:

Soon after the action with the "Merrimac," the "Monitor" anchored near the "Minnesota," off Newport News, and remained there until eight o'clock A. M. of Monday, March 10th, 1862. The "Minnesota" floated at about four o'clock A. M. of the same day and proceeded to Hampton Roads. At eight o'clock A. M. the "Monitor" got under way and steamed to Hampton Roads, arriving there about half-past nine the same morning. She was lustily cheered by the entire fleet as she steamed past the vessels.

Late on Monday night Lieutenant T. O. Selfridge took command, having been ordered by G. V. Fox, Assistant Secretary of the Navy, and three days afterwards Lieut. Selfridge was relieved by Lieut. W. N. Jeffers. From the 10th of March until the destruction of the "Merrimac" on the 11th of May, the "Monitor" laid at Hampton Roads, guarding the Elizabeth and James Rivers, and always ready for the "Merrimac." During this time her pilot-house was strengthened by heavy pieces of oak being bolted to the lower part, and covered with three layers of iron plates, each one inch thick, the surface making an angle of 40 degrees with the deck, and coming up on the sides of the pilot-house to just below the sight holes. May 8th she engaged the Battery on Sewell's Point, in company with the fleet. During this period her officers and crew suffered much inconvenience from bad ventilation, and from the sea frequently sweeping over her decks (especially at the change of tide), large quantities of water getting below.

On the 12th of May the "Monitor" led the vessels that went to Norfolk on the evacuation of that city by the rebels, and a few days afterwards proceeded up the James River as one of the flotilla under command of Commodore John Rodgers, who commanded the iron-plated steamer "Galena." On the 15th of May she participated in the engagements of Fort Darling on the James River, seven miles below Richmond, Va. This action lasted four hours. The "Monitor" was struck several times by heavy shot, but received no material damage.

From this time, until the retreat of the army from the Peninsula, the "Monitor" was employed patrolling the James River, and frequently engaged with the enemy's sharpshooters and artillery upon the banks of the river. She arrived on the 31st of August at Newport News, being the last vessel that came down the James River.

Commander T. H. Stevens relieved Lieut. Commander W. N. Jeffers from the command of the "Monitor" the latter part of July or early in August, and Commander John P. Bankhead took command of her in September. In that month the "Monitor" proceeded to the Washington Navy Yard for repairs. She sailed again for Hampton Roads in November.

On the 29th of December, 1862, she sailed for Beaufort, N. C., in company with the steamer "Rhode Island," her convoy, and on the night of the 30th she foundered near Cape Hatteras. About half of her officers and crew were carried down with her; the others escaped to the convoy "Rhode Island." The cause of her foundering is not known. It may perhaps be assigned to the fact that she had lain all summer in the hot sun of the James River. The oak timber, which had been fitted to the top edge of the iron hull, had shrunk so, that when in the heavy sea there was two or three feet of water over it most of the time, on the weather side; and the water found its way through this space and flowed in great volume into the ship, with fatal effect.

Among those of her crew lost when she foundered, was the son of our townsman, William Nicklis.

I append to this history the naval record of Rear Admiral John L. Worden, U. S. N., the commander of the "Monitor," and several testimonials of commendation for his services, from Congress, and from different Chambers of Commerce. The

State of New York presented him with a sword. Buffalo was not unmindful of the hero, some of her citizens having sent him the first testimonial he received. These testimonials could not be otherwise than gratifying to the gallant man who had, with his officers and crew, so successfully fought the first fight of the kind in the world, destroying the "Merrimac" as a fighting ship forever, and thereby saving human lives and property that cannot even be calculated. I learned out of his own mouth that the first testimonial reached him from Buffalo, and he said it was the first thing which called his attention to the fact that he had done anything meriting commendation. He said: "I was lying on my back, helpless and blind, when my good wife put into my hands the beautiful and appreciated remembrance from friends in Buffalo. I asked my wife to guide my fingers over the inscription and the names of the donors. You cannot imagine the thrill of emotion and pleasure that passed through my mind on her doing so, and when I handled the beautiful gift of your citizens."

The testimonials were as well deserved as they were appreciated. But the name and fame of this gallant Worden are inseparably connected with the "Monitor" and her glorious fight and victory, which will live forever, and be estimated at a value far beyond the eulogy of testimonials, or of silver and gold. For, what he only claimed as a repulse, or driving into Norfolk, of the disabled "Merrimac," as he deemed her, was really a substantial victory. For all practical purposes as a fighting ship the "Merrimac" was as completely destroyed as though she had been sunk in Hampton Roads in the first day's fight. This was demonstrated by her subsequent career. She was only kept for a show or semblance of power, and the gallant though misguided Tatnall well knew this when he applied the fuse to blow her up. He was convinced of her worthlessness, and only destroyed the shell from which Lieutenant Worden and his "Monitor" had taken the power.

As a matter of great interest, I will also annex a statement from our townsman, Captain James Byers, who was captured at Norfolk where he happened to be in command of the steam tug "J. B. White," in the employ of Mr. Barton, formerly of this city, at that time a contractor on the Albemarle Canal. The Confederates pressed Byers and his steamer into their service.

The waters of Hampton Roads are classic in American history. Into their shelter, from the Old World, sailed the expedition of Captain Smith, that settled Jamestown, in May, 1607, a squadron of three ships. They have afforded a safe harbor and anchorage for the tempest-tossed mariner, from that day to this. The harbor has been the theatre of many important scenes, being so close to our great Navy Yard at Norfolk. But, towering far above them all, the record of the glorious fight of the "Monitor" with the "Merrimac" commands our admiration, as of the greatest importance, not only in the affairs of this country, but to the world at large.

All honor to the names of Ericsson, Winslow, Griswold, Bushnell, Rowland, Worden, Greene and Newton, with those of all her officers and crew, not omitting the name of volunteer Stimers. These are the men that invented, built, manned and fought our "Monitor." They all deserve to be held in the highest respect by the American people; and it should never be said, as applied to them, that "Republics are ungrateful."

The names and acts of the men of the "Monitor," the "Cumberland" and the "Congress" should be cherished and recorded with those of the sailor heroes of the past, who have made the naval record of this country one of the brightest pages of its history. They showed the world that the gallant spirit which animated the breasts of Jones, Decatur, Lawrence, Porter, Perry, and the other heroes of an earlier day, had not died out, but still lived to animate our sailors when the occasion came to arouse it, as was proved later still by Farragut, Bailey, Porter and a host of other noble sailors, who added to the proud record of the American Navy.

E. P. DORR.

BUFFALO, January 5th, 1874.

APPENDIX.

STATISTICS OF THE FIRST MONITOR.

She was 124 feet long, 18 feet wide on the bottom and 34 feet wide at the junction of the armor raft with hull, and 6½ feet in depth. Her bow raked 11½ feet, stern raked 9 feet 10 inches. The armor raft was 173 feet 4 inches long over all, 41 feet 4 inches wide and 5 feet in depth. The bow projected 15 feet beyond the hull, the stern overhung 34 feet 4 inches. The side armor consisted of 5 one-inch plates 5 feet deep, backed up with 27 inches of oak. The deck armor was 7 inches of timber laid on wooden beams ten inches square; the whole covered with two plates of one-half inch iron.

The turret was 20 feet inside diameter, formed of eight-inch plates, 9 feet in height. The top was covered with railroad bars, and a plate of iron perforated full of holes for the egress of air.

The pilot-house was formed of eight-inch square bars, with corners notched log-house fashion.

The guns were placed in wrought-iron carriages.

The power consisted of a pair of steam, low-pressure engines, with cylinders forty-inch and thirty-inch stroke, placed horizontally, and operating the screw shaft by means of bell cranks.

The screw was 9 feet in diameter and 16 feet pitch.

Steam was supplied to the main engines, also turret and blower engines, from two boilers with horizontal tubes.

The keel was laid October 22d, 1861, and she was launched January 30th, at 9:45 A. M., 1862.

During the time of her construction Captain Ericsson was continually on the ground, from early in the morning till late at night.

NAVAL RECORD OF REAR ADMIRAL JOHN LORIMER WORDEN, U. S. N.

Born in the town of Sing Sing, Westchester County, New York.

Appointed a Midshipman in the Navy, from Fishkill, Dutchess Co., N. Y., Jan. 10, 1834.

Ordered to sloop of war "Erie," June 20th, 1834, and served in her on the Brazil Station until September 20th, 1837.

Served in sloop of war "Cyane" in the Mediterranean Squadron, from 7th May, 1838, until Dec. 2d, 1839.

Served at Naval School at Philadelphia, Pa., from December 23d, 1839, until the 20th July, 1840.

Promoted to passed Midshipman on the 16th of July, 1840.

Served on board store ship "Relief" in the Pacific Squadron, from Oct. 13th, 1840, until Sept. 6th, 1842; transferred to the sloop of war "Dale," and detached from her on the 23d of October, at New York, 1843.

On duty at the Naval Observatory in Washington, D. C., from April 7th, 1844, until May 28th, 1846.

Promoted to Master Aug. 13th, 1846, and on the 30th Nov., 1846, promoted to Lieutenant.

Served on board store ship "Southampton" in the Pacific Squadron, from the 5th of February, 1847, until May, 1848, when he was transferred to the "Independence," on same station; was again transferred on July 13th, 1848, to the "Warren," of same Squadron; on the 12th Sept., 1849, was ordered to the line-of-battle ship "Ohio," on same station, and detached from her at Boston, April 29th, 1850.

On duty at Naval Observatory, from October 1850, until March 15th, 1852.

Served on board the frigate "Cumberland" in the Mediterranean Squadron, from April, 1852, until 15th February, 1855, when he was transferred to the sloop of war "Levant," and detached from her in New York in May, 1855.

On duty at the Naval Observatory, from Oct. 24th, 1855, until March, 1856.

On duty at Navy Yard, New York, from March, 1856, until July 1st, 1858.

Served on board frigate "Savannah" (as First Lieutenant) in the Home Squadron, from July 1st, 1858, until Nov. 20th, 1860.

On the 6th of April, 1861, reported at Washington under orders "for special duty connected with the discipline and efficiency of the Naval Service," but finding that ships were being rapidly fitted for service, in consequence of the secession movements, asked to be relieved from that duty and applied for service afloat.

Next day (7th), at daylight, was sent to Pensacola with dispatches for the commanding officer of the Squadron off that port (orders to reinforce Fort Pickens), and reached there about 11½ o'clock P. M., April 10th. A heavy gale blowing on the 11th, could not communicate with the Squadron. The next day (the 12th) was enabled to reach it, and deliver dispatches about noon.

At 3 o'clock P. M. of same day left the Squadron, with orders to return to Washington by rail. Took the cars at 9 P. M. for Montgomery, Alabama, and on the next day (13th), at about 4 o'clock P. M., was arrested at the first railroad station south of Montgomery, to which place he was conveyed, and there detained as a prisoner of war until Nov. 14th, 1861, when he was paroled and ordered to report to the Secretary of War at Richmond, Va.

Arrived at latter place on Nov. 16th, and left there next day (17th) by order of the Secretary of War, to report to General Huger at Norfolk, Va., who, on the next day (18th), sent him under flag of truce to Hampton Roads and delivered him to Admiral Goldsborough, who, in accordance with arrangements, sent back Lieut. Sharpe, a Confederate prisoner, whose delivery to General Huger ended Lieut. Worden's parole.

Was at Naval Rendezvous at New York, from about November 20th, 1861, until the 16th of January, 1862, when he was ordered to the command of the "Monitor," and remained in her until his removal on account of the injuries received in the encounter with the "Merrimac," on the 9th of March, 1862.

Promoted to Commander, July 16th, 1862.

Was on duty at New York as assistant to Admiral Gregory in superintending the construction of iron-clads, from August 14th, 1862, to October 8th, 1862.

Commanded iron-clad "Montauk" from October 8th, 1862, until April 16th, 1863, in the South Atlantic Squadron. In her attacked Fort McAllister, on the Ogechee River, on January 27th and February 1st, 1863, and on the 28th of February destroyed the Confederate privateer "Nashville" under the guns of that fort. Participated in the attack made by the iron-clad fleet, under command of Admiral Dupont, upon the defences of Charleston, S. C., on the 7th of April, 1863.

Promoted to Captain, February 3d, 1863.

On duty with Admiral Gregory in superintending the construction of iron-clads, from April 23d, 1863, until February 2d, 1866.

Commanded steamer "Idaho" from February 1st, 1866, until May 23d, 1866, on "trial and experimental trips."

On iron-clad duty from June 2d, 1866, until August 6th, 1866.

In command of the steamer "Pensacola" in the Pacific Squadron, from the 6th of August, 1866, until May 8th, 1867.

Promoted to the grade of Commodore, May 27th, 1868.

Ordered to Naval Academy, as Superintendent, December 1st, 1869.

Promoted to grade of Rear Admiral, November 20th, 1872.

RESOLUTIONS, PRESENTATIONS, ETC.

LETTER FROM REAR ADMIRAL WORDEN.

U. S. Naval Academy,
Annapolis, Md., Dec. 22d, 1873.

My Dear Sir,—I enclose herewith copies of certain papers, addressed to me, in reference to the "Monitor" affair, viz.:

A resolution of the Senate and House of Representatives of the United States, tendering thanks, etc.

A letter of thanks from the Secretary of the Navy.

A resolution of the Assembly of the State of New York, authorizing a sword to be presented to me.

The letter of the Secretary of State of the State of New York, accompanying the sword on its presentation.

My reply to letter of Secretary of State.

And a resolution of thanks from the Chamber of Commerce of New York.

I also enclose a copy of the letter of the citizens of Buffalo transmitted with the gold box. The inscription on the box is as follows:

LIEUTENANT JOHN L. WORDEN, U. S. N.
From Citizens of Buffalo, N. Y.,
April 8th, 1862.
"You beat the 'Merrimac' and saved the 'Minnesota.'"

Description.—Between the upper lines and the motto is a picture of the fight between the "Monitor" and "Merrimac," engraved on the lid of the box.

I have no knowledge of the amount or character of the tests to which the guns of the vessel had been put; I only know that they had not been sufficiently tested to satisfy the Bureau of their endurance, and hence the order I received.*

I am, dear sir, very truly yours,

JOHN L. WORDEN.

To E. P. DORR, Esq., Buffalo, N. Y.

JOINT RESOLUTIONS OF CONGRESS.

Resolved by the Senate and House of Representatives of the United States of America in Congress assembled:

That the thanks of Congress and of the American people are due and are hereby tendered to Lieutenant John L. Worden, U. S. N., and to the officers and men of the iron-clad gun-boat "Monitor" under his command, for the skill and gallantry exhibited by them in the late remarkable battle between the "Monitor" and the rebel iron-clad steamer "Merrimac."

"SEC. 2." *Be it further*

Resolved, That the President of the United States be requested to cause this resolution to be communicated to Lieutenant Worden, and through him to the officers and men under his command.

Approved July 11th, 1872.

(Vol. 12, p. 622.)

THANKS FROM THE NAVY DEPARTMENT.

NAVY DEPARTMENT, March 15th, 1862.

SIR,—The naval action which took place on the 9th inst. between the "Monitor" and the "Merrimac" at Hampton Roads, when your vessel with two guns engaged a powerful armored steamer of at least eight guns, and after a four-hours' conflict repelled her formidable antagonist, has excited general admiration and received the applause of the whole country.

The President directs me, while earnestly and deeply sympathizing with you in the injuries which you have sustained, but which it is

---

*I had asked him if the "Monitor's" guns had been sufficiently tested before her engagement with the "Merrimac."—NOTE BY E. P. D.

believed are but temporary, to thank you and your command for the heroism you have displayed and the great service you have rendered.

The action of the 9th, and the performance, power and capabilities of the "Monitor," must effect a radical change in naval warfare.

Flag Officer Goldsborough in your absence will be furnished by the Department with a copy of this letter of thanks, and instructed to cause it to be read to the officers and crew of the "Monitor."

I am, respectfully, your obedient servant,

GIDEON WELLES.

Lieut. JOHN L. WORDEN, U. S. N.,
Commanding U. S. steamer "Monitor," Washington, D. C.

PRESENTATION OF A SWORD BY THE STATE OF NEW YORK.

STATE OF NEW YORK, ASSEMBLY CHAMBER,
ALBANY, April 23d, 1862.

On motion of Mr. Coles,—

Resolved, That the Secretary of the State cause a sword and its accoutrements, with a suitable inscription, to be manufactured and presented to that gallant son of the State of New York, Lieutenant John L. Worden, as a slight testimonial of his bravery in the late naval engagement at Hampton Roads. By order,

J. B. CUSHMAN, *Clerk*.

OFFICE OF THE SECRETARY OF STATE OF THE
STATE OF NEW YORK,
ALBANY, December 16th, 1862.

To Lieut. JOHN L. WORDEN:

SIR,—In accordance with the enclosed "resolution" of the Assembly, passed at the last session of the Legislature of the State of New York, and in behalf of the people of this State, the accompanying sword is presented to you as a memorial of your heroism and skill as commandant of the "Monitor" in the action with the "Merrimac," in Hampton Roads. You achieved a triumph there which is not surpassed even by the glories that already gild our naval renown. The timely arrival of the "Monitor" at the scene of action was of such high importance as to make the event one of the most remarkable in our annals.

The "Cumberland" and the "Congress," two of our noblest frigates, were summarily destroyed by the mailed monster. Our naval supremacy seemed utterly prostrate. The public mind was overwhelmed with the magnitude of the danger impending over us. It was in this hour of trembling solicitude, and while the appalling carnage of the previous day filled every loyal heart with anguish and humiliation, that your noble "Monitor" was permitted by a kind Providence to surmount the perils of the deep and come to the rescue. And then ensued a struggle such as never had been witnessed in naval warfare—it was between two iron-clad antagonists.

From the fleet, the Fortress and the adjacent shores thousands gazed upon the scene in painful anxiety. From morning till noon, the storm of battle continued, and the result lay trembling in the balance. But the heroic daring and consummate skill of Worden, with the genius of Ericsson, triumphed.

The "Merrimac" was beaten. The battle was won. Our fleet was secured, and cities saved from the attacks of this terrible foe. Every loyal heart was electrified with joy. Gratitude for your illustrious services was manifested in Legislative halls and in all classes of society throughout the Union.

Accept this sword, emblazoned with the record of that glorious day, as an offering from your native State, commemorative of your virtues, and as an emblem of the victory which has given you enduring fame.

With sentiments of great regard, your obedient servant,

(Signed) HORATIO BALLARD,
Secretary of State.

COMMANDER WORDEN'S REPLY.

NEW YORK, December, 1862.

To HON. HORATIO BALLARD, *Sec'y of State of State of New York, Albany, N. Y.:*

To serve our country in any hour of peril has been my highest ambition. I have looked fondly, in many distant climes, upon the emblem of her greatness, power and glory floating from the masthead, and ever with the determination that it should never be sullied if my life could avert such a calamity.

It is not surprising then, that, regarded as having won a tribute from my country and the approbation of my own gallant and patriotic State, I should feel that fame has nothing more to offer. These events, while they fill to the brim the measure of my happiness, only make me more sensible of the support which I received from the brave officers and men associated with me, and the heroism of the noble spirits who less fortunate than myself, perished in the effort to save our flag from traitors.

I am happy that the triumph to which you refer presents so grand an illustration of the great principle by which our nation is distinguished. The genius and skill of another land, fostered by our institutions, furnished the means by which, under the providence of God, I have been enabled to act a part for which, without such assistance, I would not have been qualified.

The gratitude of our country is an honor for which men, far more deserving than myself, have often struggled in vain. That this should be deemed a reward for me, is a circumstance which I cannot mention without feeling that nothing less than the aid of heaven could have produced a result so gratifying.

I am not unconscious that many of my brethren in the Navy, occupying my position, would have obtained the same end, or that thousands of our countrymen would have been overjoyed to have rendered the same assistance or service; but I hope I may be pardoned in rejoicing that the opportunity was given me to accomplish the greatest hope of my existence. For the kind manner in which you have presented this testimonial, I beg you to accept my thanks.

I have the honor to be,

Very respectfully,

Your obedient servant,

(Signed) JOHN L. WORDEN,

Commander U. S. N.

FROM THE NEW YORK CHAMBER OF COMMERCE.

CHAMBER OF COMMERCE OF THE STATE OF NEW YORK,

NEW YORK, March 26th, 1862.

Lieut. JOHN L. WORDEN, *U. S. Navy:*

SIR,—I have the pleasure of inclosing herewith a copy of resolutions complimentary to yourself, passed by this chamber on the 12th inst. Adding my hope that you may be speedily restored to your health and to the public service,

I am, with high respect, your ob'd't servant,

(Signed) J. SMITH HOMANS,

Secretary.

CHAMBER OF COMMERCE OF THE STATE OF NEW YORK,
NEW YORK, March 12th, 1862.

At a special meeting of the Chamber of Commerce this day, the following preamble and resolution were adopted:

Whereas, It is proper that this Chamber should express its approbation on occasions of great acts of heroism; and,

Whereas, Lieut. Commander John L. Worden, U. S. N., on board of the "Monitor" steam battery, then untried and just arrived from a perilous passage, engaged a vessel of war five times the size of the "Monitor," and four times her power of armament, this vessel being then engaged in the destruction of our ships of war; and,

Whereas, The "Monitor," handled with great skill and gallantry, did succeed in driving off the "Merrimac;" therefore,

Resolved, That the thanks of this Chamber be presented to Lieut. Commanding John L. Worden, his officers and crew, for the great skill and daring shown by them in the recent conflict with the rebel steamer "Merrimac."

CHAMBER OF COMMERCE,
NEW YORK, March 18, 1862.

I certify that the preceding is a true copy of preamble and resolution adopted by the Chamber of Commerce, March 12th, 1862.

J. SMITH HOMANS,
Secretary.

A GOLD BOX FROM THE CITIZENS OF BUFFALO.

Lieut. JOHN L. WORDEN, *United States Navy:*

SIR,—The undersigned, citizens of Buffalo, New York, ask your acceptance of the accompanying box, in token of their respect and admiration of the gallantry and heroism displayed by yourself, as commander of the "Monitor," in her desperate, but triumphant, conflict with the "Merrimac," in Hampton Roads, on the 9th day of March ultimo.

We sincerely congratulate you, sir, upon the good fortune which has given you a place among the heroes of your country; and we as sincerely congratulate the service to which you belong upon the laurels which it has acquired through your skill, courage and persistence.

The work of a few exciting and perilous hours has rendered your name illustrious,—"Not for a day, but for all time."

That you may speedily and completely recover from the injuries received during that terrific combat, in which your bravery was tried, as in a crucible, and found to be pure and perfect metal, is the fervent prayer of your friends and fellow citizens,

DEAN RICHMOND,	MILLARD FILLMORE,	WM. G. FARGO,
E. P. DORR,	ALEX. W. HARVEY,	WM. MONTEATH,
FRANK PEREW,	JOHN ALLEN, JR.,	R. WHEELER,
H. E. HOWARD,	J. N. DORR,	WM. B. PECK,
R. C. PALMER,	D. P. DOBBINS,	A. J. RICH,
JOHN L. JEWETT,	JASON PARKER,	GEO. C. WHITE,
E. W. ENSIGN,	H. A. FRINK,	C. ENSIGN,
GEO. W. HOLT,	JAMES D. SAWYER,	B. MONTGOMERY,
J. M. RICHMOND,	A. T. BLACKMAR,	G. B. GATES,
THOS. D. DOLE,	A. SHERWOOD,	L. H. RUMRILL,
J. M. GWINN,	P. L. STERNBERG,	MYRON P. BUSH,
D. S. BENNETT,	JOHN H. VOUGHT,	SHELDON PEASE,
O. L. NIMS,	A. W. HORTON,	WM. PETRIE.

H. B. FLEMING, Capt. U. S. A.

BUFFALO, N. Y., April 8th, 1862.

NOTES REFERRING TO THE "MONITOR."

BY ALBAN C. STIMERS.

There were two engines 40 inches diameter of cylinder by 26 inches stroke of pistons.

When the fires were managed with skill, the engines would make 80 revolutions per minute, and the vessel eight knots an hour in smooth water. Six knots was, however, her common speed.

Left New York harbor on the 6th day of March, 1862; weather fine, with a fresh wind, so much so that as soon as we were outside of Sandy Hook the sea washed over the deck so deeply that it was not considered safe to permit the men to go on deck, the top of the turret only being available. This was 20 feet diameter by 9 feet high.

The next day there was a tremendous gale with a high sea running. There were two wooden gunboats with us as convoys; these rolled so much that when they rolled from us we could see under the bilge, and when toward us, could see down the main hatch. The motion of the "Monitor" was so easy and quiet that a glass inkstand stood upon a polished mahogany case on the table in the Captain's cabin during the entire voyage without slipping. The sea washed over the deck, however, in the most terrific manner; the only inconvenience from this was that the water came down the air pipes which supplied the blowers, causing the belt to break and the stoppage of the blowers; also, causing the gases of the furnace fires to flow out of the ash-pan doors into the engine room and thence throughout the vessel, driving all hands to the top of the turret. The steam went down and the engines were stopped during four hours. Many of the firemen and all the engineers were so asphyxiated that the lives of some of them were despaired of.

During the night following, the wire wheel-ropes came off the wheel and all hands were occupied most of the night in steering, by hauling on the ropes by hand, and getting on the wheel again.

On the morning of the 8th, and during the day, the weather was calm and the sea smooth. At two P. M. we heard the guns of the "Merrimac" in her conflict with the wooden vessels, and as we approached at night could see the broadsides of fire. We surmised correctly the situation, and cleared for action, expecting the enemy would come out on her way North, a trip we intended to prevent if it was in our power.

We arrived off Fortress Monroe at nine o'clock in the evening of the 8th, and the Captain and myself spent the evening on board the "Roanoke," as she was commanded by the senior naval officer present in those waters, Captain Marston. There we learned the state of affairs, and went up to Newport News and anchored near the frigate "Minnesota," which was aground, and which we were ordered to protect from the assaults of the enemy the next morning. We finally anchored there at two o'clock A. M. of the 9th.

The guns on the "Monitor" were Dahlgren, eleven-inch shell guns, weighing 16,000 pounds each. There were two. We threw cast-iron solid shot, spherical, weighing 168 pounds each, with a charge of 15 pounds of powder.

The engagement commenced at eight o'clock in the morning and lasted until one o'clock in the afternoon. We were struck twenty-one times, eight times on the side armor, twice on the pilot-house, seven times on the turret, and four times on the deck. None of these were injurious, except one of those on the pilot-house; this broke one of the iron beams of which it was formed, and placed the Captain *hors de combat.*

He was the only person wounded, though several were knocked down by leaning against the inside of the turret while a shot from the enemy struck the outside in the vicinity. I was one of these, but as I was only touching my hand, I immediately jumped up again, while those who were leaning their shoulder against it were senseless for a couple of hours, and then greatly excited during a couple more.

Very truly yours,

ALBAN C. STIMERS.

STATEMENT RELATING TO "MERRIMAC," ETC.

BY CAPTAIN JAMES BYERS.

Captain James Byers, of Buffalo, N. Y., was at Norfolk from Sept., 1860, to the 8th day of May, 1862, Master of steam tug "J. B. White," built at Buffalo by Geo. Notter. He was employed by the contractors building the Albemarle Canal. The "Merrimac" was sunk by the Federals near the Navy Yard, previous to the evacuation of Norfolk, to avoid her falling into the hands of the Confederates. She was raised for the Confederates by Baker Bros., wreckers, and put into the dock at Norfolk, cut down and fitted up—a heavy frame of wood covered with heavy plate iron. They worked on her night and day. She was armed with four heavy guns on each side, one on bow and one aft—ten heavy guns in all.

She went out on Saturday, the 8th of March, 1862, under command of Admiral Buchanan, and sunk the "Cumberland" and "Congress" on that date. I saw the fight from the deck of my steamer. She also exchanged shots with the "Minnesota," which was aground on the middle ground in Hampton Roads, half way between Sewell's Point and Newport News. The "Merrimac" could have easily destroyed the "Minnesota" on Saturday (March 8th), but they did not wish to harm her—she would be too valuable to them as a prize. They felt sure of her on the morrow, with all the other craft in the "Roads" and at anchor off Fortress Monroe.

The "Merrimac" retired for the night, and anchored off Sewell's Point until next morning. In her encounter with the "Cumberland" and "Congress," a shot from one of the guns of the "Cumberland" entered the muzzle of the bow gun of the "Merrimac," bursting the gun and killing seven men.

Sunday, March 9th, the "Merrimac" hove up and steamed out to "finish up" the work of destruction and capture left undone the day before. The day was clear and pleasant, the sun shining brightly, with little or no wind. Some Confederate officers and citizens of Norfolk came on board my steamer at Norfolk, and ordered me to get under way and run out to see the "Merrimac" finish up. We ran down off Craney Island, and from our deck saw the fight between the "Monitor" and "Merrimac." The Confederates were all in high spirits, anticipating an easy victory. They talked very freely over the mission and marked programme of the "Merrimac." She was to capture the "Minnesota" and all the vessels in the Roads, and then to proceed to New York and other Eastern cities. There was no doubt about the result, and that she would go where she wished, with impunity to herself.

We had been off Craney Island about half an hour, in plain sight of Hampton Roads and the different craft there. We saw the "Merrimac," and presently the "Monitor" came out and attacked her. We could not tell what the "Monitor" was—nothing had ever been known of her in Norfolk, and it was all speculation what she was. The fight was watched with great interest. Soon there began to be doubts about the result. Some Confederate officers who had been down nearer than we were, came back, and in passing told us that the unknown craft was a "*wicked thing*," and we better not get too near her. One of the shots from one of the combatants came skipping over the water very near us, from nearly a mile distant.

We stayed there until the fight was over. The "Merrimac" came back into the river badly disabled, and almost in a sinking condition. Tugs had to be used to get her into the dry dock at the Navy Yard, the crew pumping and bailing water with all their might to keep her afloat. I saw her in the dock at Norfolk next day, was on board of her and made a personal examination of the ship. The effect of the "Monitor's" guns upon the "Merrimac" was terrible. Her plated sides were broken in, the iron plating rent and broken, the massive timbers of her sides crushed; and the officers themselves stated that she could not have withstood the effect of the "Monitor's" guns any longer, and that they barely escaped in time from her.*

The "Merrimac" lay in dry dock repairing and strengthening for six weeks, when she was again put afloat under the command of Admiral Tattnall. After the "Merrimac" was repaired and came out of dock, the only thing she did was to form part of an expedition to go out into the Roads to attempt to capture the "Monitor." The expedition was

---

* This was the time when the "Monitor" retired a few minutes to get some more shot from below into the turret.—NOTE BY E. P. D.

made up of the "Merrimac" and two tugs, manned by thirty volunteers on each tug-boat. They were all armed and provided with iron wedges and top mauls and tar balls. The plan was to board her, a tug on each side landing the men, and throwing lighted tar balls down through the ventilators and wedge up the turret so it would not revolve. They took my steamer as one of the boats, but I refused to command her or go with her. The "Monitor," luckily for them, did not come out over the bar to give them a chance to try the experiment. The pounding which the "Monitor" gave the "Merrimac" the latter never recovered from. They lost faith in her.

I ran the blockade on the 8th day of May, 1862, escaping with my steamer, the "J. B. White," to Fortress Monroe, where I met President Lincoln with some of his Cabinet, giving him the first information he had of the true state of affairs at Norfolk, and the preparations made by the rebels to evacuate it.

Admiral Tattnall blew up the "Merrimac" off Craney Island shortly afterwards—a fitting end to a gallant but unfortunate ship in the service she was last engaged in.

JAMES BYERS.

www.ingramcontent.com/pod-product-compliance
Lightning Source LLC
Chambersburg PA
CBHW031810090426
42739CB00008B/1232
* 9 7 8 3 3 3 7 0 1 0 9 7 3 *